For Those Wandering Along the Way

For Those Wandering Along the Way

Ryan Diaz

RESOURCE *Publications* • Eugene, Oregon

FOR THOSE WANDERING ALONG THE WAY

Copyright © 2021 Ryan Diaz. All rights reserved. Except for brief quotations in critical publications or reviews, no part of this book may be reproduced in any manner without prior written permission from the publisher. Write: Permissions, Wipf and Stock Publishers, 199 W. 8th Ave., Suite 3, Eugene, OR 97401.

Resource Publications
An Imprint of Wipf and Stock Publishers
199 W. 8th Ave., Suite 3
Eugene, OR 97401

www.wipfandstock.com

PAPERBACK ISBN: 978-1-6667-1655-9
HARDCOVER ISBN: 978-1-6667-1656-6
EBOOK ISBN: 978-1-6667-1657-3

08/23/21

To my wife Janiece.
I am yours, now and always.

I have never separated the writing of poetry from prayer.
I have grown up believing it is a vocation, a religious vocation.

—Derek Walcott

Contents

Preface | ix
Acknowledgments | xi
For Those Wandering Along the Way | 1
To Wanderlust | 2
The Long Defeat | 3
All Is Well | 4
The Black Christ | 5
A Liturgy for This Present Moment | 6
Elfreth's Alley | 7
Sir Dregil and the Beasts of Wice | 8
To Oberon | 13
To the Sunflower | 14
To Sabbath | 15
After Dark | 16
Weary Hands | 17
Holy Saturday | 18
Justice and Mercy | 19
Morning | 21
Category 5 | 22
Playing with Fire | 23
The Dust Bowl | 24
America: A Eulogy | 25
Timber | 27
The Standing Stones | 29
Zoom Fatigue | 30
El Sordo | 31
An Invocation for Illumination | 32
Snowfall | 33

To Death | 34
The Poet's Mantra | 35
Dread | 36
All Hallows Eve | 37
Christmas Eve | 38
O Holy Night | 39
A Threshold Prayer | 40
Death Masks | 41
On the Parish Steps | 42
Amen | 43
The Victorious Dead | 44
Apokalypsis | 45
To the Saints | 47
Ex Nihilo | 48
On the Magic of Reading | 49
The Holy Present | 50
To My 1948 Hermes Baby | 51
A Morning Liturgy | 52
Upon Hearing Her Diagnosis | 53
Christ in Paradox | 54
To My Ebony Churchwarden | 55
With Unveiled Faces | 56
Eden's Heralds | 57
Abel's Blood | 58
Ash Wednesday | 59
There & Back Again | 60
Eden in the Grey | 61
The Radiator | 62
Tobacco | 63
To Malcolm | 64
Springtide's Eve | 65
Perspective | 66

Preface

I RANG IN THE New Year unemployed and depressed. I was a shell of my former self, an automaton that resembled the living. I was going through the motions. Every day I'd wake up, say my prayers, fill out job applications and take up residence in front of the TV until my wife called me for dinner. I'd eat, clear my place, and was soon off to bed to begin the process all over again. I tried to spin it, convince myself that was all ok, but while my smile worked on friends and family, deep down inside, my faith was waning. What was once a blazing hearth was reduced to a few stalwart embers fading in and out of life.

I had been here before. The dark night of the soul wasn't new to me. But this time, something was different. My usual tips and tricks came up hollow and empty. Prayer and scripture felt dead on my tongue and lifeless in my ears. The faith I once had, unbeknownst to me, had been subtly replaced with a cold, brutal cynicism. Prayer failed because I questioned more than I prayed. Scripture ceased to soothe because it no longer blew me away. God was distant because I had put up my arms in defense, sealed the doors, and for good measure wrapped it in yellow caution tape. I had lost my capacity for wonder, my faith was hollow, and I was spiraling.

In the midst of all this, I did something I did not expect, I began to write again. I had always dreamed of being a poet, a man of letters, but life and, quite frankly, a poor theology of vocation led me to put down my pen. Yet there I was, jobless, with nothing to lose, and so with much fear and trembling, I picked up a notebook and put pen to page.

Poetry saved me. Grace used each pen stroke to soften my stony heart and enliven my embittered soul. With each line, I felt

Preface

more myself again. I finally understood King David. The Psalms were his lifeline. These poems were mine.

Dear Reader, I present you with the product of a thawing heart. Read each poem with care. Let them work on you. God works in the grey and through the subtext. This is why he often speaks in poetry. Poetry speaks when reason is at a loss for words. I pray reading these poems will do for you what writing them did for me.

Yours Truly,
Ryan Diaz

Acknowledgments

Ekstasis Magazine
In Parentheses
Wingless Dreamer
Tempered Rune Press
Bearings Online

FOR THOSE WANDERING ALONG THE WAY

These are the songs we sing on the way;
Through valley-glades and desert moors,
Across chaos-waters to distant shores,
In the dead of night with frosty chill,
Across sun-scorched earth and hardened clay,
These are the songs we sing on the way.
Taught to us by mothers old,
Glimmering bright with gilded gold,
Words woven from the ancient spells,
Knit together with Psalms, we pray,
These are the songs we sing on the way.
Mortal tales of eternal life,
A chance of hope amid the strife,
A beacon found on ancient fells,
In the twilight just before the day,
These are the songs we sing on the way.
Sung aloud with notes of liberation,
Sounding like a prophet's declaration,
All things new, all things well,
Winter always breaks for May,
These are the songs we sing on the way.
A candle burning mid the black,
Guiding us with faded maps,
Till we stumble through the door
And find a bed on which to lay,
These are the songs we sing on the way.
Take up now thy holy words,
Hum with me this sacred dirge,
Hold it deep within your soul,
For when you don't know what to say,
These are the songs we sing on the way.

TO WANDERLUST

With the wind I travel
Along the sea I ride
Soaring on the desert winds
Till I come to Neptune's pride.

I accompany the mariners
Adventurers with swords
To cities resplendent
And in dark cavernous hordes.

I stir the fire deep within
I call to cities grey
Arise, arise, O' Venturer
Ignore the calls to stay.

Find me on the narrow road
Outside your mother's door
They say you'll put your life at risk
But friend, what is living for?

THE LONG DEFEAT

Welcome son, to the long defeat,
The battle at the edge of time.
What do you see out in the bleak?
Things left untold in rhyme.

Arm yourself with guard-blade and shield,
And march onward into the fray.
When the fell things howl don't you yield
If you long to taste a new day.

Who is our foe? Father, tell me.
Who shall I face at march's end?
Is their armor thick, do they flee
Or do they stand and never bend?

Son, I cannot say lest you break
But for now I'd savor your breath.
For the enemy comes with haste
And brings with him our last foe, DEATH.

ALL IS WELL

In the still of dawn just before the morn
In the quiet solitude all is well;
Just before the sun shimmers on the lawn
And the birds begin to echo like bells.

I listen as creation tells it's tale,
The wind whistling like a bard;
It sings the song of ancient days untold
And lands unknown, lost in the deep-wood far.

There the green is still vivid with virtue
The lion lays with the lamb and makes peace
The old paths still lead to places unseen
And grapes are heavy with wine for a feast.

But as the sun rises higher it fades
The resplendent radiance turns to dark;
I return to where reality holds sway
And so I must etch the dawn in my heart.

In the quiet solitude all is well
And the birds begin to echo like bells.

THE BLACK CHRIST

I gaze upon the Black Christ, darkened by the—
Soot of petitions, the incense of—
Bodies and souls and soiled robes. Prayers that—
Have stained Christ's face over the years. Prayers—
Whispered and woven with gallons of tears,
Confessions, regrets, laments and silence,
Bathing him, a holy baptism,
Blackening his marble effigy.
I gaze upon the Black Christ, darkened by the—
Sins committed against black bodies and
The violence that tears families a—
Part of me wonders if he hears the sound—
Or in solidarity does he bare—
For all to see the sign of his person,
Blackened and battered, whipped and beat and mocked,
Evidence of his divinity and
The realization that blackened bodies—
Bear the *Imago Dei*, his dignity.

A LITURGY FOR THIS PRESENT MOMENT

How long O' Lord, the choir sang,
Their voices heavy with drear;
Notes robbed of angelic flair,
Their incense tinged with despair.
The sun-laden walls were dark
And even the bells refused—
To sway, lest they ring of cheer.
Stained glass turned to muted grey,
Their colors drained like blood from veins.
And all the while the choir sang,
How long O' Lord? Lord how long?

ELFRETH'S ALLEY

I stumbled upon a road cobbled with stone,
The ancient kind, bearing the marks of time.
It winded it's way to a red brick home,
Hidden just behind a forest of vines.
I carefully pushed through a black iron gate,
Which creaked and groaned with rust and misuse,
Into a courtyard, old, walled and wooded,
Where warm beams of day never left their place.
Here was a space untouched and untroubled,
A sanctuary for the weariest soul,
Left down an alley, away from it all,
A place out of time where one could grow old.
I found myself on that cobblestone road
Looking and longing for my abode.

SIR DREGIL AND THE BEASTS OF WICE

A Commuter's Tale

I. Mondag

Off into the fray he went
Armed with naught but his wits
Down into the deep descent
A charge, a push, a blitz.

On iron steed through the dark
Dregil rode to face the beast
Dodging foe's fiery darts
Lest he become the feast.

But alas came the final blow
Hark, the creatures cry
Knight victorious over foe
He held it's head up high.

Thus was conquered Mondag along with all her fiends
Until Tiw arose to avenge her fallen queen.

II. Tiw

Tiw let out a mighty roar
Yet Dregil stood his ground
Assailed with chains of leaden ore
The knight was tied and bound.

Heavy was Tiw's oppressive yoke
Ever nigh drew death with his defeat
But in his heart hope's ember stoked
Till it's blaze burned hot and chains grew weak.

The sun rose high above the dark
Sir Dregil summoned all his might
His sword cleaved through the demons heart
Robbing Tiw forever of her fight.

Spent but victorious Dregil sheathed his golden sword
But off in the distance rang Woden's feral chord.

III. Woden

Woden sat enthroned on high
As Dregil began his deadly climb
Wreathed by ravens was the sky
Heralds of death, their master's sign.

The wind beat Dregil against the cliff
Pummeled about by ice and rain
On icy stone he lost his grip
As Woden's ravens laughed and sang.

Alas he met his one eyed foe
The battle waged on heaven's peak
Wearily his sword swung slow
At Woden's laugh the stars grew bleak.

Suddenly upon the wind came his maiden's call
And with a final push he watched Woden fall.

IV. Thun

Thunder cracked and sky was split
As Thun descended from the heights
With hammer blows the sky was lit
A display of violent light.

Dregil charged into the breach
Unafraid of wind and flame
Mjolnir knocked him to his feet
Dregil's sword-arm hung limp and lame.

Thun stood upon the fallen knight
And roared with all his pride
But pride had always been his blight
And a hidden dagger pierced his side.

Wounded still with blade in hand
Dregil prepared his final stand.

V. Frigga

Cast into the valley-shade
Dregil waited for the test
With his blood his soul was paid
He longed for bliss and rest.

Yet Frigga rose from the deep
To meet him at the pass
To rob him of dream and sleep
The two foes met at last.

Guardian, she stood with spear
At the door to peace
Wielding his greatest fear
His life she sought to cease.

Great was the sound of their clash
They lit the night with flame and flash.

VI. Father Saeturn

Blood flowing from his veins
Frigga's body laid limp against her post
His mind muddled by the pain
Dregil was leaking life and hope.

Along came Father Saeturn
Who saw the wounded man
And with great concern
Tended him with gentle hand.

Days passed into weeks
And slowly Dregil was revived
Strength returned to his feet
His soul once again alive.

Saeturn's rest had healed his scars
And so Dregil sought his maiden far.

VII. Lady Sunedai

He came upon a summer grove
flowers danced among the fields
The smell of baking leavened loaves
A banquet set with drink and meal.

Then she appeared eyes aglow
Glorious to the senses
Walking with the deer and doe
Dregil let down his defenses.

He ran into his maidens arms
She received him with a kiss
He was rejuvenated by her charms
And his heart was filled with bliss.

But as the sun hid its face
She faded into mist and again began his race.

TO OBERON

Delicate were the lips of Oberon.
His tongue was crafted with rhythm and rhyme.
Each word he spoke was melodious song,
Dripping with amber and frozen in time.
I looked for Oberon in the green-place,
In his cathedral of oak, elm, and willow.
Empty was his throne and gone was his grace.
Missing were the ravens, the doves, and the dow
The glen weeps over you, her fallen dane,
Where are you Oberon, so fair and true.
The wood begins to fade without your reign.
Return, O' Oberon and bring your dew.
Without you, Titania is but stone.
Without you, the green is no longer my home.

TO THE SUNFLOWER

Beautiful is your head that wears the crown
A wreath of golden sunlight shining bright
Carried by the slender nape of your neck
Nestled upon your laurels and tresses.
You are Apollo's child, bright from the womb
A celestial body descended—
To dwell amongst mortal men, always gazing
Enamored and allured by your body.
Across from me you sit, silent and brooding
Watching and waiting, hoping for rescue
To be plucked from your prison and taken—
Back to your father's throne in the heavens.
But as you wait, I watch your sunlight fading
Drained of your warmth, the solar hues within
Until slowly, your crown slips from your head
Joining Apollo's children amongst the dead.

TO SABBATH

Time stands still,
Day merges into night
And no one can tell the difference;
It's Friday and Sunday all at once,
Blending into one perpetual Saturday.
Rising takes on new meaning;
Rising no longer means doing
But instead ushers us into being.
Here we find resurrection,
Imbued with the Paschal energy of empty tombs;
Calling forth our weary souls,
Begging us to live again
To embrace the stillness
And learn again to be,
To embrace the pregnant pause
And once again begin to breathe
This is Selah,
The space between,
That elusive time we rarely find
And always lament to leave.

AFTER DARK

The streets were quiet, save for a hum—
The gentle buzz of fluorescent street lamps,
Singing in chorus with the night-flies and moths,
Twirling and spinning as if in a dance.
I stood there, silent in the light of the dim,
Watching as the city turned to a dream;
The night reviving those who slept in the day
And joining the dance they started to sway.
Out came the alley-cats playing their jazz,
With the strays stepping in time to the bass—
As the vagabonds watched, taking shots to the face,
Drinking each round like it was their last.
The last call came with the rays of the sun,
the dancing ceased when the street-lights went out.
There I was, on the street corner alone,
Regretting that I called the day my home.
I asked my neighbor if he saw what I saw
He shrugged and said all he heard was a hum;
The gentle buzz of fluorescent street lamps,
"Though I awoke last night longing to dance."

WEARY HANDS

"I look to the hills, for whence comes my help,"
He muttered beneath the silent pass,
Gazing upon a moonless heaven,
Contorting his hands as if at a mass.
Frayed knees met the wet and hallowed ground
As his dirty hands reached out for the host,
hanging, waiting, suspended in air,
For a sign, a touch from the Holy Ghost.

HOLY SATURDAY

Dark and cloudy was that fateful Saturday;
Heavy were her eyes, filled to brim with dismay,
Cold was the chill that ran along her spine,
Bloody were her knees as she kneeled to pray—

And shut was the maw of the of that white washed tomb,
Polished marble shining in the dim light's gloom.
There she sounded prayers, silent and raging,
Seeds watered with tears, desperate to bloom.

Her hair was damp, rain nestled on her crown,
Brighter than all the earthen jewels in-ground.
The heavens adorned her in radiant light,
Creation groaned, joining her in breathless sound.

Grief laid her to rest on a bed of dew
And as she slept she dreamt that her seeds grew;
Flowers growing up from that white washed tomb,
Arraying its walls with splendorous hues.

She awoke to the sun sneaking over the hill;
Juvenile beams of light asserting their will,
Warming her face, she felt the touch of a hand,
And together they danced in the daffodils.

JUSTICE AND MERCY

Dedicated to Breonna Taylor;
on the day she was denied Justice.

The gavel bangs. The sound rings
hollow and empty, robbed of its weight
Justice sounds superfluous,
it's power for the few, for power
remains with the few and so justice rings
hollow for the many.
And those who hallow its name
in fact profane and curse
their very object of worship.
For the god that they worship
is no god at all.
It bears the trappings of God,
it sounds like God,
but it is not God;
for God's name is Justice
and Justice has been denied,
spat on and shattered,
demonized, vilified,
God is unrecognized. Nor is his cry,
"JUSTICE and MERCY!"
They reply,
"LAW and ORDER!"
They deny,
they distract,
they dismiss
the God who cries with those who cry,
"JUSTICE and MERCY!"

The Father cries,
"JUSTICE and MERCY!"
The Son cries,
"JUSTICE and MERCY!"
The Spirit cries,
"JUSTICE and MERCY!"
The Faithful cry,
"JUSTICE and MERCY!"
When will THEY give HER
Justice and Mercy?

MORNING

I awake to clinking and clashing plates,
The soft pitter-patter of quiet feet
And the song of a bird perched upon my gate,
Whistling away with notes tender and sweet.
I awake to the scent of black coffee,
Brewing and bubbling in its cauldron-pot,
Beckoning me to rest in its black sea
While its elixir works to wake my thoughts.
I awake to embrace the warm sun's rays—
As they nestle upon the edge of my skin,
Calling out to me from beyond my haze
Where the dark hides Apollo's gleaming grin.
But when I awake, will I see you there?
Crowned by the sun, your scent and song so fair.

CATEGORY 5

Behold the rain and tempest beating down;
A storm surging with roaring wicked howls,
Clouds converging over this hallowed ground,
But behind these walls we are safe for now.
This cabin we built, a home here for two,
Tucked away in a grove between the peaks.
Assailed by summer's heat and winter's blues,
Still it stands, its walls neither crack nor creak.
But can it stand the rain that pours without,
Can these walls we built hold back the wind?
Or does this dreadful gale put us to rout,
And will the lightning leave all burnt and singed?
But we've been here before, this too shall pass,
For this home we built, we built to last.

PLAYING WITH FIRE

O' sing my soul purified by fire;
Immolated beneath her blazing gaze,
Burned by the sound of her harp and her lyre.

She cut my cords, my bonds, and wires,
Freeing me from my gold gilded cage,
O' sing my soul purified by fire!

Her sheets were kindling, her bed a pyre
And there we dared to channel her rage,
Burned by the sound of her harp and her lyre.

Her voice rung out like an angelic choir
And I never tired of singing her praise.
O' sing my soul purified by fire!

To live up to her, I could never aspire,
Instead I was singed by the heat of her blaze,
Burned by the sound of her harp and her lyre.

Who could stand what she requires
And yet I long for the warmth of her rays.
O' sing my soul purified by fire,
Burned by the sound of her harp and her lyre.

THE DUST BOWL

They were trampled in the trenches,
Sinking beneath the mud and mire,
Choked out bodies
And burnt out souls,
The refuse of war,
Left behind as carrion for crows.
And they are us,
Those with spirits crushed
Beaten and battered and shattered,
Hollow human husks—
Groaning,
Groaning for liberation;
For the sweet dew—
To soak through
And make dirt out of dust,
Turning souls into soil.
We are creatures—
Created for cultivation.
Not this,
Whatever this is called.
This,
This thing we call life
Or death,
Or the grey doldrums between—
Where seeds refuse to grow.
We're groaning
And groaning,
Desperately dancing for rain,
Demanding the dew to revive us again.

AMERICA: A EULOGY

November 3, 2020: Judgement Day

either way, today—
america dies,
or at least it begins to writhe—
with democracy's death pangs,
choking on that vomit we dare call—
LIBERTY.
the guillotine is prepped,
sam has bared his neck
and while the ignorant cheer,
his head will roll.

damn our idiocy!
damn our pundits and profiteers
and armchair analysts!
damn the right,
damn the left!
they lit the flames
and then wondered why cali is burning,
their sacred sites set aflame,
they point fingers at each other
and yet change spit behind our backs,
counting the profit with their false prophets.
damn them all!

the reaper calls the coroner—
to give his apocalyptic diagnosis;
this is the end,

we burned it to the ground,
and now we're dancing in the ruins,
painting our faces with ashes,
blind to our burning,
celebrating our "progress."

TIMBER

The axe is at the root
of this old oak
we named Democracy.
Long has it stood;
sown in the fires
of revolution,
cultivated and pruned
at the cost of human lives.
Tall it grew
till it bloomed
with the blossoms of liberty,
enduring fire and flame
and the deep chill
of tyranny's winter.
Tall has it stood;
unswayed by
wind and rain
and all manner of storm.
Its boughs grew thick
and strong,
its canopy
a covering
for lost
and wayward sons
looking for
liberation,
to feast on the fruit
from its eaves.

But now,
the axe is at the root,
the blade is bared
and that old oak
which withstood
all manner of hell
now sees its end
in the eyes of those
who long ago
sowed its seed.
The axe is at the root,
its hilt is in our grip.
The axe is at the root,
waiting for a fool to yell
timber.

THE STANDING STONES

I stumbled upon the standing stones
Laid in neat rows in the forest's clear;
White heads emerging from the broken earth,
Crowned with moss and the decay of years.

Each one seemed to be carefully laid,
Their distances all measured with care
And each stone seemed about the same,
Though they looked different from the weather's wear.

I laid between them on the dew-dipped grass
And felt myself sinking through the dirt,
As if the stones were pulling me down—
To the treasure they hid beneath the earth.

There I saw over what the stones stood watch;
Long chests measuring about my height
And in them were souls long damned,
Buried under the earth's eternal night.

Then it dawned me as I lay there—
That the plot in which I laid was empty
And the chest bore a name I knew all too well;
This standing stone was laid for me.

ZOOM FATIGUE

All we have are shadows,
faintly flickering
on this old, cold, lifeless
stone. All we have are lies,
faint impressions, distorted
reality. And we
are chained here helpless,
playing shadow puppets,
pretending, playacting,
willfully ignorant.
For we know that this, this
is unreality,
a vague impression of truth,
shadow and vapor and
vanity. Vanity,
all this is vanity,
a cheap trick of Socrates,
shadows and light and lies.
This is our existence:
We are souls chained in rows,
longing to face the sun,
to see the world we left behind
before we were
shackled by shadows.

EL SORDO

The darkness settled in with the pain,
All he could hear was the deep thrum of death
And the demonic vitriol of facist scum,
Calling down tongues of fire like rain.

The sky was blue: a glimpse of God's eye,
An eternity just before the end.
And as he stared into the sun he knew;
Glorious are those who laugh when they die.

AN INVOCATION FOR ILLUMINATION

O muse, O heart, O Spirit guide—
Me to the world between our dreams and day,
Give me eyes to see the veiled, shrouded way;
Where glory is hidden and meaning breathes,
Where spirits, sprites, and all good things reside.

O muse, O heart, O Spirit lead—
Me by the path untrodden and wide,
Take my hand, over my steps abide;
Less I waver to wander astray,
Blind to Mystery and all her good deeds.

O muse, O heart, O Spirit, I—
Call upon you to unveil my eyes.

SNOWFALL

The spell sets in with the powder,
Conjured on the heights of heaven—
By an old mage's frozen song;
Forged with runes and Ullr's blessing,

Turning suburban streets into—
A scene from an old nordic tale,
Bathing all in white celestial glow;
The home of winter's hidden vale.

TO DEATH

I know one day we are destined to meet—
At the end of the road where the sunshine sets,
But can we please postpone our ordained greet,
So that you might receive me free of regret.

THE POET'S MANTRA

Do not go a day without—
creating, making or shaping;
Turning words into woven wonders
And terrestrial terms into celestial lights.

Never let the ink run dry,
Let it flow,
Till all the canvas is carved—
With ink and spirit
And all the truth that has gone unsaid.

Do not be silent,
With the voice of your Father—
SPEAK
And call forth the Word—
Who will give you words when the ink is dry
And your voice is quiet.

Be still now,
Let the words come,
They will come.
It may take time.
Don't rush,
Be still.
Listen for the still small voice,
The whisper on the wind,
And then, when you hear it,
Say something true.

DREAD

There is a fear that quiets the inner man,
A still dread felt deep within the bowels.
It's always there, a persistent whisper,
A whistle you can't seem to silence,
Always there like a shadow in the sun.
And I can't seem to shake it or name it,
But all I know is that I feel it—
Deep within, just underneath the skin,
When you walk in the room with that look on;
And one wonders if this is the end.

ALL HALLOWS EVE

This feels like the bottom of the bottle;
the manic musings of madmen—
conjured up to plague the conscious.

This feels like a pit in your stomach
with the density of a collapsing star;
pulling all into its endless abyss.

This feels like a kitchen knife between the ribs,
slowly sliding into place;
guided by the hand of a lover.

This feels like the end,
a cataclysm,
an unholy apocalypse;
a cool kiss on your crown—
placed by her cheating lips,
candy coated with lies—
To disguise the sting.

This is what it feels like—
to have your heart blown to bits.
This is what it feels like—
to be the poor sap who was tricked.

CHRISTMAS EVE

We lie here beneath these bundles of baubles,
Nestled around the fire in the pale moonlight
And all is quiet. And so are we,
Looking for the words to make this right.

O HOLY NIGHT

The bell sang it's song with notes of brass and bronze;
A haunting tune on a winter's eve.
As the snow inked white the trees and its leaves—
The bell tolled cold, chanting winter's song.

And I could feel each toll, the crash and the bang,
It sounded like dusk and starless skies.
As I walked it followed me with its cry,
Dancing on the wind each time that it rang.

Then it was silent and the air stood still
And even the snow seemed frozen in place,
For there it was an emblem of grace,
A solitary star on heaven's sill.

A THRESHOLD PRAYER

We are on the edge of the threshold;
The thin space between what is and what could be,
Ignorant of what lies beyond, scared
To lose all that we will have to leave behind.

We are on the edge of the threshold;
Our feet frozen in place, unwilling to step,
To cross from the dawn and embrace the dusk,
Learning to love the moon's silver light.

We are on the edge of the threshold;
Though it's quiet, we are not alone,
But he who is himself a threshold—
Stands as bridge and guide to the other side.

We are passing over the threshold;
From the past into the infinite surreal,
The holy of holies, the hidden place,
Where colors are brighter and time stands still.

DEATH MASKS

We have a face we only wear in death,
More real than the one with which we—
Lived. For the living never see—
The true us while we have breath,
The veil falls when we have none left.
In death's grim box, we lie bare,
Stripped of pretense, nothing to wear.
Nothing to hide, we are unmasked.
We are most true here at the pass—
When we put on our Death Masks.

ON THE PARISH STEPS

"Mother Mary full of grace."
He uttered on the steps.
A river ran down his face,
But Mother Mary left.

Orphaned by the angels,
He found comfort in a noose.
Found dangling by strangers,
A display of bloody truth:

Sinners look for comfort,
Devils seek reward,
Sons beg for mothers,
Daughters die by the sword.

AMEN

Born on a bedside
Nursed in the dark
Forgotten in the morning
Hidden in the heart.

Shared like a secret
Screamed in despair
Sung like a song
No sound fills the air.

Carved out of questions
Stitched with a hope
Shaped by the faith
Of men trying to cope.

THE VICTORIOUS DEAD

Trembling members
Weathered hands
Crawling to the cross
Just there at the finish line
Where wins look like a loss
Surrounded by
saints and martyrs
Fools, pimps, and popes
We close our eyes
Scared to death
With nothing but a hope.

APOKALYPSIS

It's all in the subtext.
The things unsaid.
The things unprayed.
The things unread.
It's hiding beneath the topsoil.
Nestled just out of reach,
Between lines,
Implied,
In the quiet before you speak.
It's all in the subtext.
It's in the pause.
Frozen in amber.
Robbed of kinetic energy.
Waiting for release.
It's all in the subtext.
The meaning we seek.
Hidden behind truth and lies.
Just underneath our skin,
Waiting for emancipation,
For revelation,
For Apocalypse.
It's all in the subtext.
Between stanzas and verses,
Between blessings and curses.
Between who you are,
Who you want to be,
And who you're meant to be.
It's all in the subtext.
The real nestled behind reality.
Providence and destiny.

It's all in the subtext.
Peeking between Hallelujahs.
Smothered with Amens.
It's in the letters you didn't send.
It's all in the subtext.
The regrets,
The maybes,
The could have beens,
The breakups,
The abandoned friends.
It's all in the subtext.
What you meant to say,
What you didn't.
What your meant to pray
What you didn't.
It's all in the subtext.
Between the lines on the page.
In the pause before words.
In the storm.
In the rage.
It's all in the subtext.

TO THE SAINTS

Where have all the heroes gone,
The heroes of the faith?
The Clements
The Augustines
The Thurmans
The Yeats.

Saints of old with rod in hand,
Who cut the ancient paths.
So tired souls,
Longing for home,
Could find the hearth at last.

Where have all the heroes gone,
The heroes of the faith?
The Brigids
The Avilas
The Julians
The greats.

Saints with eyes to see the sun
And the promised land.
So tired souls,
Begging for sight
Might find a guiding hand.

Where have all the heroes gone,
The heroes of the faith?
On and on heavenward
To leave us in their place.

EX NIHILO

Day 1

Void; all black and all encompassing void,
Chaos incarnate, O eternal night,
Hear the voice of He who sits above all,
Who expands beyond even your expanse;
The great is and was and ever will be.
Hear me, O primal dark, you are alone—
No more. Be filled with glory resplendent,
Your twin brother called to shine in your shade
and hold all in his hands while you slumber.
Together you are the hands of time.
Night behold day, chaos meet order;
Brothers eternal, forever standing guard,
Always keeping the cosmos in balance:
Moon and sun, servants of the eternal son,
Reflecting his glory forever—
So that all might gaze and praise his name,
The Word spoken, who gave you your being
And who is your source and light and life.
Bound forth in his name, fill the heavens full,
Till all see the wonder of Day and Night.

ON THE MAGIC OF READING

I got lost one day in a wood of words;
A forest found only in pages turned
And as I wandered something stirred,
A fire lit, that for some time hadn't burned.
The leaves told tales that I had never heard
And their runic song caused my heart to yearn—
for visions of lands long left unseen,
glimpsed, only with shut eyes, when one dreams.

THE HOLY PRESENT

We are all perpetually pacing,
Our gnarled fingers betray our anxious hearts.
Our minds are perpetually racing,
Seeking what the future hides in the dark.
We are enslaved to the immediate,
We desire to know what can't be known.
We worship the god of expedience
And bear on our troubled shoulders his throne.
But a voice cries out to us on the wind,
"Be still, take a breath and pause, be still and
Know that I calm the storms, without and within,
Be still and know, take true SHALOM from my hand,
For only in my sacred presence—
Can you truly know the Holy Present."

TO MY 1948 HERMES BABY

These keys are pregnant with stories to tell
And the ink is soaked through with memory,
In them the long forgotten past still dwells—
Longing to be pried free from the page's shell,
Rescued from the den of obscurity,
These keys are pregnant with stories to tell.
Who will hearken to their ancient spells,
Who will drink deeply of their revelry.
In them the long forgotten past still dwells,
Deep in the bowels of their bardic wells—
A song from eons past longs to be free,
These keys are pregnant with stories to tell.
And as I type, the words rise like the swells
And I am guided by their mystery,
In them the long forgotten past still dwells.
Listen for the knell of the carriage bell
And the steady percussion of iron keys,
For these keys are pregnant with stories to tell,
In them, the long forgotten past still dwells.

A MORNING LITURGY

It starts with a cup of coffee;
Two sugars and a splash of milk—
Tenderly turned with a silver spoon
And while I sip and savor,
I sink into my chair's embrace—
As the sun awakes from its slumber.
There I am joined by Keats and Yeats
And I savor their words between
Savory sips of vigilance.
And it's here in this moment,
When the sun shines through the panes
And their words still sit on the tip of my tongue,
That it dawns on me;
This is a sacred moment,
A sacrament, a liturgy,
An unspoken litany,
A holy moment disguised—
In the guise of ordinary,
Hidden, a sacramental vision,
Heaven, waiting for discovery.

UPON HEARING HER DIAGNOSIS

Will I still be me when I forget my name,
When my eyes can see but my mind is blind,
When words lose their sense and cease to sound the same
And when I forget all my own is mine?
Will I still be me when I forget you,
When the sound of your name doesn't ring a bell,
When your face is replaced by a stranger's,
When you have to chant your name like a spell?
Will I still be me when my body decays,
When I'm imprisoned by bedside visits,
When my feet no longer carry my weight,
When all my freedom and motion is gone?
I will still be me, in your memory—
But, only if you remember me.

CHRIST IN PARADOX

The God of Golgotha;
Enthroned on a skull.
The conquering king—
With a crown of thorns.
The perpetually loved
And forsaken son.
The eternal God,
Who made flesh his home
And learned to reign
By giving up his throne.

TO MY EBONY CHURCHWARDEN

There you slumber, my black briar dragon,
Waiting to breathe golden roses of heat
And spew forth your terrible ashen spawn
Till all is filled with the grey of your speech.
You are ever my constant companion,
My dim ember in the marauding dark,
An ever vigilant battalion,
An undying, never yielding spark.
But there, you sit, waiting for me—
To pick you up and awaken your heat,
To summon your flame with spark and tree,
Till once again you begin to speak,
Till all the room is filled with dancing whisps,
When I draw you near my expectant lips.

WITH UNVEILED FACES

For now we see dimly;
A tree is a tree,
The sunset
The simple
Passing of time,
The water's edge
Is but a boundary,
The moon, the sun's
Reflected shine.
But put pen to page,
Add voice to song
And watch the alchemy transform,
Unveiling nature's hidden face:
The touch of eternal dimly veiled.
Then the tree becomes
A world its own.
The sunset,
A portal,
A thin space between,
The water's edge,
A chasm unknown
Beckoning explorers
To discover her deep,
The moon a fair maiden,
Waiting for rescue,
Fleeing from dawn,
Longing for dusk.
For now we see dimly,
Barely piercing the veil
Longing to see with faces unveiled.

EDEN'S HERALDS

Let us bear the sun to the unsunned spots
And carry the green to the dead dark wastes.
Let's sing Pan's sweet spell and expel the rot,
Lets ride with the dawn to give the dark chase.
For we are luminary heralds,
Earthen vessels brimming with solar dew,
With thumbs green as iridescent emeralds
And minds spry as a canopy of yew.
We are the vine-born, the Green Man's children,
Raised from the clammy claws of ash and dust,
Washed in living streams whose source is hidden,
Animated with the Spirit's winds and gusts,
Empowered to extend Eden's borders—
So that all might bathe in her holy waters.

ABEL'S BLOOD

The blood soaked soil sings—
The song of the innocent,
It cries through dust
Filling the earth,
Soaking the dirt,
Beckoning us to hear—
The whispers of its word.
Will we listen
Or deaf pass by?
Humming a song of ambivalence,
Willfully ignorant
Of the song of the innocent.

ASH WEDNESDAY

Today I'll take the ash upon my brow,
Signed with a cross and whispered words of dust.
Marked as I am I wander about—
Looking for those, who like me, have been touched.
Our eyes meet in silent prayer, our heads bow—
In brief acknowledgement. We are dust-born,
Raised from the earth with water and vow,
Crowned now with laurels instead of thorns.
For now, we must assume the palm's embers
And wear this frame woven through with carbon,
But each day after we will remember—
That we were made for glory and gardens.

THERE & BACK AGAIN

My toes dangle over the doorways edge;
A riverbed of possibility,
Beckoning me to leave safety's ledge
And chart a course through her tributaries.
But I am anchored to this place called home,
My heart belongs to the heat of the hearth.
And though part me longs to wander and roam,
There's no place like her in all of the earth.
But maybe I'll leave, just for a while,
Roam the roads with neither compass or map,
Collecting dirt, dust, friendship and miles—
Till I can't picture her and long to turn back.
Then, I might learn to see her with new eyes,
At the end of the road, just on the rise.

EDEN IN THE GREY

I came upon a grove
Nestled between a crack in the pavement,
A green glen hidden in a city of grey,
Alive with rushing rivers,
Wet with heavenly dew,
A small piece of Eden tucked away.
Safe from the overgrowth of metal,
Vines of copper and lead,
Behemoths of steel and iron,
A wasteland of asphalt—
Black and all consuming.
I longed to live in that Eden,
To feel its cool winds and clear waters,
The soft touch of its green fields,
And the shade of its trees and their leaves.
But deep down I knew
All I would do
Was bring the wasteland with me.

THE RADIATOR

All I could hear that morning
Was the squeal and pop
Of the radiator
As it rumbled and roared
Out of its long slumber,
Letting off angry hisses
As hot steam searched
For a way to escape.

It lumbered there in the corner
Inanimate yet alive;
A still dragon curled and waiting
A totem of fire and heat
Hephaestus' forge
Nestled between the sofa and bar cart,
Curiously out of place
In our New York apartment.

TOBACCO

I hold a pinch of two-tone tobacco,
Leaves dried ochre and black, smelling sweetly
Of a warm fall morning in September.

I mash the kindling into my briar bowl
And attempt to strike a light in the wind,
Cupping the delicate flame in my hands.

It takes two matches and a long draw to
Get the smoke going, releasing the Autumn
Wind caught in its leaves, turning winter into

A warm fall morning in September.

TO MALCOLM

Priest, prophet, poet. Spell-scribe and sonnet singer,
The hymn writer, great Herbert's legacy,
Inkling and ink weaver, God's Psalm spinner.
The grey haired green-man, England's memory.
John Donne's disciple, heaven's holy bard,
A wizened shepherd for the weary soul,
A nightingale singing under twilight stirred,
A light post, a lamp, a burning bit of coal.
Pipe-craver, smoke blower and ash tamer,
A warm hearth for the stranger you call friend.
Pen wizard, sage teacher and place namer,
A silver tongued truth teller, a true godsend.
Heaven's poet, guised in rock and roll,
Sharing with us the Word found in words old.

SPRINGTIDE'S EVE

First comes the rain,
The last sigh of winter
Reluctantly releasing its grip
On Apollo's mare.

Then comes the blue,
Sapphires piercing through the veil
Drawing nebulous curtains
across the heavens,

Revealing sleeping buds
And subtle hints of green
Buried under the drab brown
Of winter's refuse.

And every morning
As it draws near
I hear the sound of rumbling
And stones turning,

The air smells like incense,
Empty tombs, and resurrection,
The first signs and first fruits
Of long days and short nights.

The air is thick with new birth,
with gardens and redemption.
Winter belongs to Friday,
Spring blooms with Sunday.

PERSPECTIVE

Why did we replace Heaven with Space?
A world of wonder displaced, ousted by
The inky black of a vacuous void.

When did our language lose its luster
And why did our silver tongues cease to stir?
Pentecostal flames snuffed out by reason,

Mechanized minds blind to what lies beneath
The accidents of creation. Essence,
Hidden under substance, bounded and sealed,

Desperately waiting to be revealed
And seen. For though it lies behind a veil
We can still see in part and sing its song

But only if—we have ears to hear
And eyes to see and willing lips ready
To call the expanse by its true name, Heaven.

www.ingramcontent.com/pod-product-compliance
Lightning Source LLC
Chambersburg PA
CBHW071742040426
42446CB00012B/2435